GREEN CRAFTS

Cool Crafts
with
Old T-shirts

by Carol Sirrine

green projects for Resourceful Kids

CAPSTONE PRESS
a capstone imprint

Snap Books are published by Capstone Press,
151 Good Counsel Drive, P.O. Box 669, Mankato, Minnesota 56002.
www.capstonepub.com

072010
005900R

 Books published by Capstone Press are manufactured with paper
containing at least 10 percent post-consumer waste.

Library of Congress Cataloging-in-Publication Data
Sirrine, Carol.
   Cool crafts with old t-shirts: green projects for resourceful kids / by Carol Sirrine.
   p. cm. — (Snap books. Green crafts.)
   Includes bibliographical references and index.
   Summary: "Step-by-step instructions for crafts made from old T-shirts and information about
reusing and recycling" — Provided by publisher.
   ISBN 978-1-4296-4009-1 (library binding)
   1. Handicraft — Juvenile literature. 2. Salvage (Waste, etc.) — Juvenile literature. I. Title.
II. Series
TT157.S5284 2010
745.5 — dc22   2009033263

Editor: Lori Shores
Designer: Juliette Peters
Production Specialist: Laura Manthe
Photo Stylist: Sarah Schuette
Project Production: Marcy Morin

Photo Credits:
All photos by Capstone Studio/Karon Dubke except:
Carol Sirrine with Liam, 32; Shutterstock/Amy Johansson (chain link fence design element);
Shutterstock/Ian O'Hanlon (recycling stamp design element)

Capstone Press thanks ArtStart in St. Paul, Minnesota, for its contributions
to the projects included in this book.

Essential content terms are **bold** and are defined at the bottom of the page
where they first appear.

Table of Contents

8

10

12

16

20

24

Introduction

When it comes to protecting the planet, everyone can help. Every day you can choose to follow the three Rs of caring for the environment: **reduce**, reuse, and **recycle**. It's not hard to make the world a better place. Many people help reduce waste by buying products with less packaging. You probably recycle at least one thing every day. And reusing old items can actually be fun! Thrifty crafters have found ways to reuse items and keep them out of the trash. With a little creativity and a few craft supplies, you can turn trash into treasures.

Trendy Ts

Today T-shirts are like walking advertisements for everything from sports teams to rock bands. But originally T-shirts were only worn under men's dress shirts. In the 1930s, both men and women started wearing T-shirts as casual wear. Soon T-shirts were dyed bright colors and printed with images and messages. The T-shirt is definitely one trend that has stood the test of time.

reduce — to make something smaller or less

recycle — to make used items into new products

T-Shirt Terms

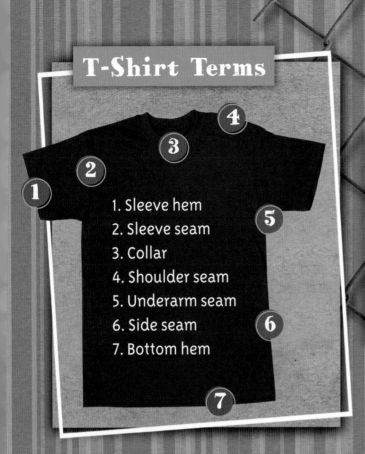

1. Sleeve hem
2. Sleeve seam
3. Collar
4. Shoulder seam
5. Underarm seam
6. Side seam
7. Bottom hem

Go Metric!

It's easy to change measurements to metric! Just use this chart.

To change	into	multiply by
inches	centimeters	2.54
inches	millimeters	25.4
feet	meters	.305
yards	meters	.914

Everywhere you look, people are wearing T-shirts. Maybe you're wearing one now. But what happens when you're ready to say good-bye to your old T-shirts? Actually, you never have to say good-bye, because your old T-shirts can gain new life as different, useful items. You can turn them into works of art, handbags, or even rugs!

The projects in this book are only a taste of what you can do with old T-shirts. Once you get started, you will come up with more ways to reuse your favorite T-shirts and keep them out of a **landfill**. And you can feel good knowing you're doing your part to save the environment — one T-shirt at a time.

landfill — an area where garbage is stacked and covered with dirt

Picture Perfect

When you outgrow a great T-shirt, give it new life by making it a work of art. Show off your favorite T-shirt by framing it and displaying it in your bedroom. Show your school spirit by framing your school T-shirt. Or honor your favorite band. With so many T-shirts to choose from, your room will be filled with style.

Here's what you need:
- **T-shirt, any size**
- **frame, large enough to fit image**
- **chalk**
- **fabric scissors**
- **1 piece of cardstock, cut to fit frame**
- **masking tape**

1

2

Step 1
Lay the T-shirt flat on a table or cutting surface. Remove the back of the frame and the glass. Center the frame over the image on the T-shirt.

Step 2
Use chalk to draw a line along all four edges of the frame.

Step 3
Cut along the chalk lines. Save the extra material for another project.

Step 4
Lay the T-shirt image over the cardstock, making sure image is centered. Fold the extra fabric to the back of the cardstock. Use masking tape to tape down the edges.

Step 5
Place the glass back into the frame. Put the image into the frame and reattach the back.

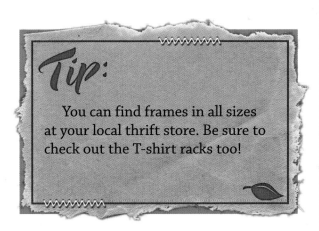

Tip:

You can find frames in all sizes at your local thrift store. Be sure to check out the T-shirt racks too!

T-bone

Got a pet that likes to chew? With T-shirt T-bones, even your pet pooch can go green. A tug toy made from old T-shirts is sure to be a hit with your dog or the dog next door. Just braid, knot, and get ready for some tug-of-war with man's best friend.

Here's what you need:
- 1 large T-shirt, or more for different colors
- fabric scissors
- ruler
- masking tape

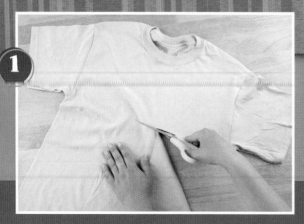

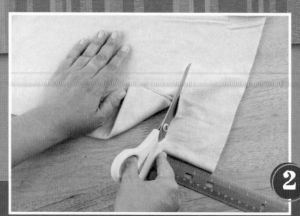

Step 1

Lay the T-shirt flat on a table or cutting surface. Cut off the bottom hem. Cut off the top of the shirt just below the underarm seam.

Step 2

Fold the T-shirt in half so the folded edges meet. Use a ruler to measure 3 inches from one cut edge. Cut across the fabric to make a 3-inch strip, making sure to cut through all layers.

Step 3

Unfold the strip. Cut off both side seams to make two strips. (If your T-shirt didn't have side seams, cut both ends of the loop.) Gently pull on the ends of each strip to stretch and curl the fabric.

Step 4 *(not pictured)*

Repeat steps 2 and 3 until you have 10 strips. Save the extra strip for another project. To add different colors to your braids, use different T-shirts or scraps from other projects.

Step 5

Use masking tape to secure the ends of three strips to a table. Braid the strips tightly and secure both ends with masking tape. Repeat two more times.

Step 6

Hold all three braids together and tie a tight knot in one end. Tightly braid the three braids together and make another knot at the end. Remove the masking tape from the ends of the small braids.

Tip: Don't have a dog? You can still get in on the fun by making toys for the local animal shelter.

How to Braid

Lay three strips side by side. Cross the left strip over the middle strip to the center. Then cross the strip on the right over the new middle strip. Repeat, alternating left and right strips.

On the Go

Girls on the go know that a good carryall bag is a must-have accessory. Here's a bag you can grab on your way out the door. The perfect size for your wallet, cell phone, and a notebook, this bag can hold them all. But whether you're off to the library or meeting friends at the mall, this bag will come in handy again and again.

Here's what you need:
- 1 T-shirt, any size (heavyweight shirts work best)
- fabric scissors
- fabric glue
- straight pins
- needle and thread
- dinner plate (optional)
- chalk (optional)

How to Sew by Hand:
Slide the thread through the eye of the needle. Bring the ends of the thread together and tie a knot.

Poke your threaded needle through the fabric from underneath. Pull the thread through the fabric to the knotted end. Poke your needle back through the fabric and up again to make a stitch. Continue weaving the needle in and out of the fabric, making small stitches in a straight line.

When you are finished sewing, make a loose stitch. Thread the needle through the loop and pull tight. Cut off remaining thread.

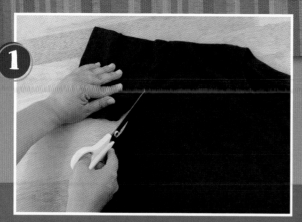

1

Step 1
Remove the sleeves by cutting ½ inch from the outside edge of the armhole seams. Be sure to leave the seams on the T-shirt.

Step 2
Turn the shirt inside out. Apply a thin line of fabric glue ¼ inch from edge around armholes. Fold edges over and press flat.

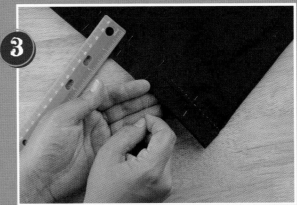

Step 3
With the shirt still inside out, line up the bottom hem and pin closed. Sew along the hem about 1 inch from the edge with small, tight stitches.

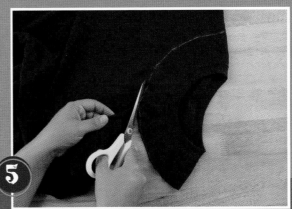

Step 4
If the neck hole is too small for the opening of the bag, lay half of a dinner plate over the collar. Draw a line around the plate with chalk.

Step 5
Cut along the chalk line, making sure to cut through both layers of the shirt. Glue the edge down to make a finished edge as in step 2. Let dry.

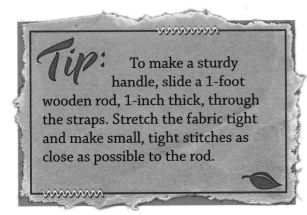

Tip: To make a sturdy handle, slide a 1-foot wooden rod, 1-inch thick, through the straps. Stretch the fabric tight and make small, tight stitches as close as possible to the rod.

Chill Pillow

Whether it's a late night studying or a long chat on the phone, these pillows will help you chill out. For a different look, **stencil** a word or phrase on a pillow with fabric paint. Or sew on felt shapes with embroidery thread. Make as many as you want — you can never have too many pillows!

Here's what you need:
- **1 T-shirt, any size**
- **ruler**
- **chalk**
- **fabric scissors**
- **straight pins**
- **needle and thread**
- **pillow stuffing**

1

2

Step 1

Lay the T-shirt flat on a table or cutting surface. Use ruler and chalk to draw a rectangle ½ inch larger on all sides than you want the pillow to be. If using a shirt with an image, be sure to center the image in the rectangle.

Step 2

Cut along the chalk lines. Save the extra material for stuffing the pillow.

Step 3

Put right sides together, making sure to line up the edges. Use pins to join edges.

Step 4

Sew edges with small stitches about ½ inch from edge. (See sewing instructions on page 10.) Leave a 4-inch opening in the middle of one edge for stuffing.

Step 5

Turn pillow right side out and fill with leftover T-shirt material and pillow stuffing.

Step 6

Sew the opening closed with tiny stitches.

Tip: To reuse even more, save scraps from your other T-shirt projects to use as stuffing for your pillows.

stencil — to paint over a piece of plastic with a design cut out of it to transfer the design onto a surface

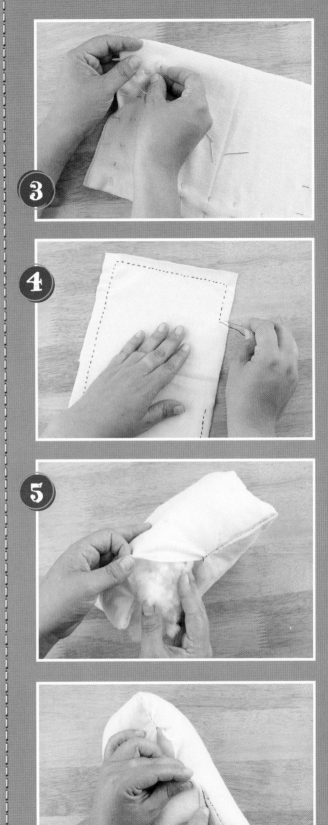

Fast and Fabulous

Here's a bag that is quick to make and fun to use. Simply snip, sew, and thread a string through the collar of your shirt. Voilà! A perfect drawstring bag! These bags are great for holding small items when you're out and about. They also make stylish gift bags!

Here's what you need:
- 1 T-shirt, any size
- ruler
- chalk
- fabric scissors
- straight pins
- needle and thread
- safety pin

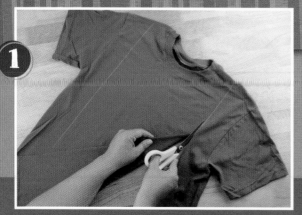

1

2

Step 1
Lay the T-shirt flat on a table or cutting surface. Use a ruler and chalk to make vertical lines from the shoulder seams to the bottom hem. Cut along chalk lines.

Step 2
Make a horizontal line above the bottom hem, making the bag as long as you want. Add ½ inch to the length for the seam. Cut along line.

Step 3
Turn the T-shirt inside out and line up the edges. Pin edges together and sew with small, tight stitches about ½ inch from the edge. (See sewing instructions on page 10.)

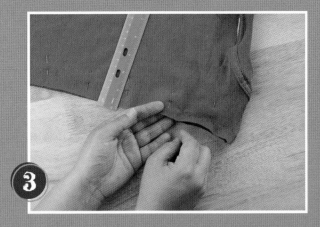

Step 4
Cut a strip of leftover fabric about 1 inch wide and 12 inches long. Pull on the ends of the strip to make it curl into a tube. Attach a safety pin to one end.

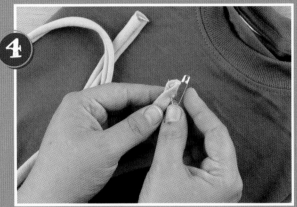

Step 5
Turn bag right side out. Cut a small hole on the inside of the collar.

Step 6
Push the pin and strip through the hole and around the collar to make the drawstring. Remove pin. Trim ends of drawstring and tie together.

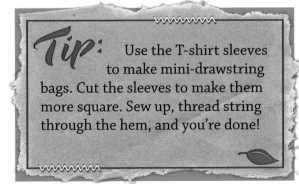

Tip: Use the T-shirt sleeves to make mini-drawstring bags. Cut the sleeves to make them more square. Sew up, thread string through the hem, and you're done!

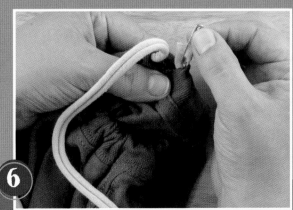

T-yarn Scarf

Scarves add style to any fashion trend. For this scarf, start with super-soft yarn from old T-shirts. T-yarn is great for knitting, crochet, or any other way you use yarn. Use T-yarn to make this chic scarf. It can also be made into a headband, a belt, a dog leash — you name it! Once you start finger weaving with T-yarn, you won't want to stop.

Here's what you need:
- **T-shirts without side seams or images**
- **ironing board**
- **fabric scissors**
- **needle and thread (optional)**

Step 1
Lay the T-shirt flat on an ironing board and cut off the bottom hem.

Step 2
Slide the T-shirt onto the narrow part of the ironing board like a tube. Make a diagonal cut from the bottom edge until you have about 1 inch in width. Begin cutting a strip of fabric about 1 inch wide all the way to the edge of the ironing board.

Step 3
Rotate the T-shirt on the ironing board and continue cutting the 1-inch strip. Continue rotating shirt and cutting in a spiral to make one long, continuous strip of fabric.

Step 4
When you reach the underarm seam, make another small diagonal cut to release the strip of fabric.

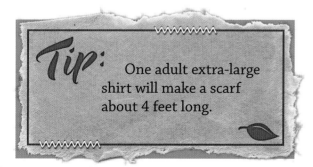

Tip: One adult extra-large shirt will make a scarf about 4 feet long.

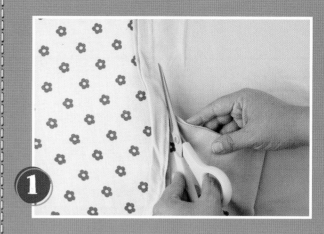

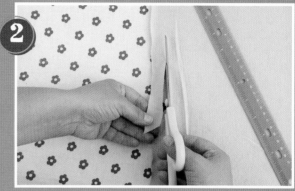

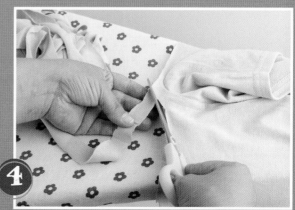

To finish this project, turn to the next page. ⇨

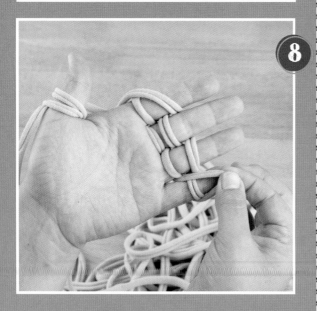

Step 5

Take about 1 foot of the strip in your hands and gently tug to stretch and curl the fabric. Work your way down the strip, pulling each 1-foot section.

Step 6 *(not pictured)*

Repeat steps 1 through 5 to make more T-yarn as needed.

Step 7

Wind the end of the T-yarn around your thumb two or three times. Weave the yarn through your fingers starting behind and ending in front of your index finger.

Step 8

Weave yarn around fingers again so you have two loops on each finger. Lift the bottom loops up, over, and off each finger to the back of your hand. You will have one loop left on each finger.

Step 9

Continue weaving and lifting off loops, occasionally tugging on the tube forming behind your hand. You can unwind the T-yarn from your thumb after you've lifted loops off your fingers a few times.

Step 10

When you reach the end of the yarn, you can attach more yarn by sewing the ends of strips together.

Step 11

When the scarf is as long as you want it, cut the T-yarn, leaving a 6-inch tail. Thread the end through the remaining loops on your fingers and pull tight. Tuck the ends of the T-yarn inside the tube.

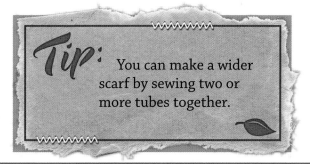

Tip: You can make a wider scarf by sewing two or more tubes together.

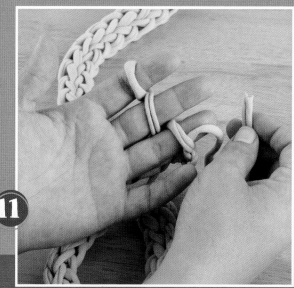

Kickin' Kozies

You don't have to go back to the 1980s for a great pair of leg warmers. No matter the weather, leg warmers are sure to make a style statement. Worn with skirts or jeans, these recycled T-shirt leg warmers will get you noticed.

Here's what you need:
- 1 large T-shirt, at least 18 inches wide
- ruler
- chalk
- fabric scissors
- 2 safety pins
- needle and thread

Step 1

Lay T-shirt flat on a table or cutting surface. Use ruler and chalk to mark a 14-inch by 18-inch rectangle, using the bottom hem as one of the long sides. Cut along chalk lines, making sure to cut through both layers.

Step 2

Separate the fabric so you have two pieces. Fold the pieces in half lengthwise with right sides facing in. Line up the long edges and pin closed. Sew the pinned edges together with small stitches about ½ inch from edge. (See sewing instructions on page 10.)

Step 3

Turn right sides out and lay one leg warmer flat with seam on left side edge. Fold the seamed edge over 1 inch. Make very small cuts every inch on the new fold, not including the hem. Make sure to cut through all layers. Repeat with the second leg warmer.

Step 4

Cut two 1-inch by 36-inch strips from leftover fabric or scraps from other projects. Pull the ends of the strips to stretch and curl. Attach a safety pin to each end of one strip.

Step 5

Lay the seam flat so you can see the holes along either side. Using a strip you cut in step 4, lace up the sides of one leg warmer like an athletic shoe, starting at the hemmed edge. Repeat with other leg warmer and remove pins.

Step 6 *(not pictured)*

You can adjust the fit of the leg warmers by pulling the laces tighter or making them looser. Pulling the laces tight at the top will help them stay up.

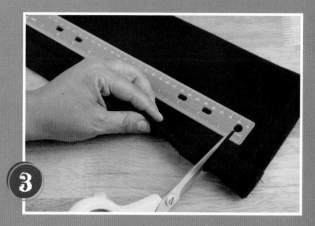

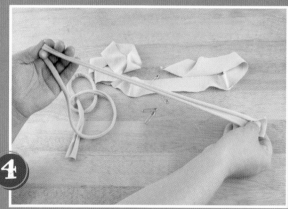

Tip: For cozier leg warmers, try using an old sweatshirt.

Undercover

A day at the beach is a great way to catch some rays. But too much sun can be bad for your skin. When you're not in the water, throw on a swimsuit cover-up made from old T-shirts. You'll be comfortable, cool, and ready for some fun in the sun.

Here's what you need:
- 2 large T-shirts
- fabric scissors
- ruler
- chalk
- needle and thread
- 2 safety pins

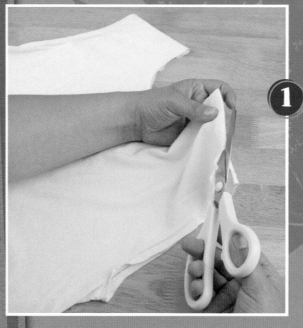

Step 1

Shirt one: Remove the sleeves by cutting along the outside of the sleeve seams. Be sure to leave the sleeve seams on shirt. Cut off the collar and shoulder seams.

Step 2

Shirt two: Cut off the top of the shirt just below the underarm seams. Cut off the bottom hem. Cut two 9-inch strips from the hem to make the shoulder straps.

Step 3

Open shirt one and lay the back piece flat, right side down. Pin one strip on the shoulder edge so that it overlaps by 1 inch. Fold the shoulder fabric on the left and right over the strip and sew with small stitches. (See sewing instructions on page 10.) Repeat on other shoulder edge.

Step 4

Put the shirt on and pin the straps to the front shoulders so that the cover-up fits. Remove the shirt and fold shoulder fabric over front straps as in step 3. Sew pieces together with small stitches.

Step 5

Turn both shirts inside out. Overlap the edge of shirt two and the bottom hem of shirt one. The hem of shirt one should be on the inside, so it shows on right side when worn. Pin pieces together all the way around. Sew with small stitches just above the hem of shirt one.

Step 6

Turn cover-up right side out. Make a cut from the bottom edge almost to the stitches from step 5. Measure ¾ inch and make another cut. Gently tug the strip to stretch and curl. Repeat all the way around the bottom.

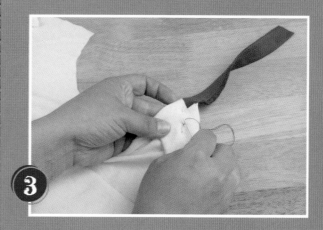

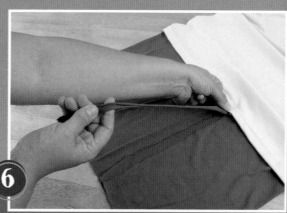

A Unique Twist

Here's a twist on an old classic. The braided rug dates back to the 1600s, when people reused old rags to make rugs. To give this rug a modern look, use strips of colorful T-shirt fabric for your braids. Make the rug as large or small as you like. The more strips you braid, the larger your rug will be. Place it under a favorite chair or beside your bed. Don't be surprised if your pet chooses it as a comfy place to sleep!

Here's what you need:
- old T-shirts
- ruler
- chalk
- fabric scissors
- needle
- nylon thread
- masking tape
- iron

Step 1
Lay T-shirt flat on a table or cutting surface. Use the ruler and chalk to draw a line from top to bottom of the T-shirt. The line should start where the shoulder seam meets the sleeve. Repeat on other side. Draw another line straight across just under the collar.

Step 2
Cut along chalk lines, making sure to cut through both layers of the shirt. Cut off bottom hem.

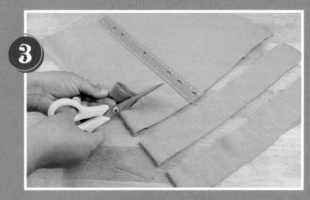

Step 3
With both layers of fabric still together, fold in half so bottom edge meets collar edge. Cut 2-inch-wide strips from folded edge to cut edge, making sure to cut through all layers.

Step 4
Overlap the ends of three strips. With a needle and nylon thread, sew the ends together.

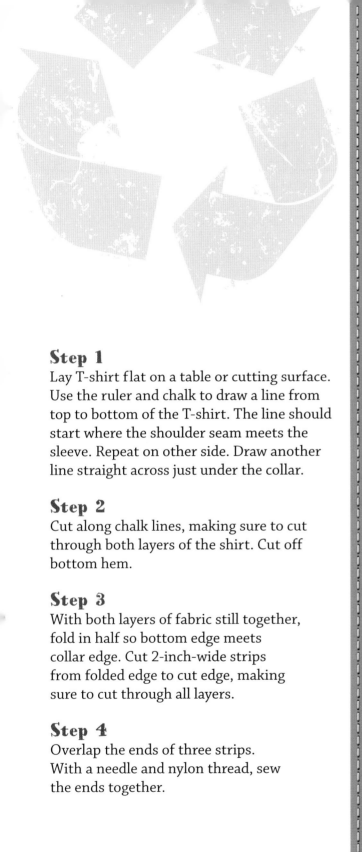

To finish this project, turn to the next page. ⇨

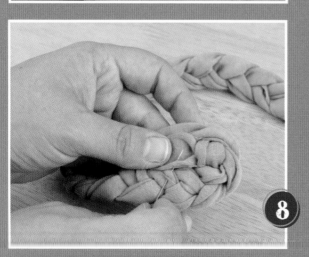

Step 5
Tape the sewn ends to a table. Braid to the end of the strips. (See braiding instructions on page 9.)

Step 6
Overlap the end of the braid with the ends of three new strips and sew together. Braid the new strips of fabric and sew the ends to three new strips again.

Step 7 *(not pictured)*
Continue braiding and sewing until you have a long braid. If you're not sure your braid is long enough, coil it around itself to see how big the finished rug will be.

Step 8
Wrap one end of the braid around itself to form a center coil. With needle and nylon thread, secure the coils with small stitches.

9

Step 9

Make another coil by wrapping the braid around the first coil. Join the sides of the coils by making one small stitch every ½ inch.

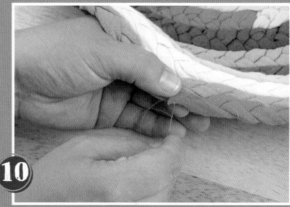

10

Step 10

Continue to coil and sew until the rug is as large as you want it to be. Twist the end of the braid flat and sew it to the last coil.

Step 11

With an adult's help, press the rug flat with an iron.

Tip:

If you make thinner strips, you can make smaller projects such as coasters or placemats.

11

Green Crafting Facts

🐞 Many T-shirts are made of cotton, a natural fiber. Natural fibers are **biodegradable**, which means they will break down in a landfill. Other T-shirts made of a cotton and polyester blend don't break down as easily.

🐞 Many nonprofit thrift stores accept old T-shirts as long as they are in usable condition. They sell the T-shirts to the public. The money from the sales goes to help people in need.

🐞 When printed T-shirts end up in the landfill, they present a large problem. Many of the inks used are bad for the environment. Eventually the inks **pollute** the soil or flow into rivers and streams.

biodegradable — able to break down naturally in the environment

pollute — to make something dirty or unsafe

When thrift stores receive T-shirts that are too worn-out to resell, they send them to "rag sorters." The rag sorters recycle cotton T-shirts into wiping and polishing cloths.

What can you do with all the scraps from your T-shirt projects? That is, of course, if you're not saving the scraps for other projects. Call your local recycling center to find out if T-shirt material is accepted. If not, they may be able to help you find a fabric recycler near you.

Glossary

biodegradable (by-oh-dee-GRAY-duh-buhl) — able to break down naturally in the environment

embroidery thread (im-BROY-duh-ree THRED) — string used to sew designs on cloth

environment (in-VY-ruhn-muhnt) — the natural world of the land, water, and air

landfill (LAND-fill) — an area where garbage is stacked and covered with dirt

pollute (puh-LOOT) — to make something dirty or unsafe

recycle (ree-SYE-kuhl) — to make used items into new products; people can recycle items such as rubber, glass, plastic, and aluminum.

reduce (ri-DOOSS) — to make something smaller or less; people reduce waste by throwing away fewer items.

stencil (STEN-suhl) — to paint over a piece of plastic with a design cut out of it to transfer the design onto a surface

Read More

Rodger, Ellen. *Recycling Waste.* Saving Our World. Tarrytown, N.Y.: Marshall Cavendish Benchmark, 2008.

Ross, Kathy. *Earth-Friendly Crafts: Clever Ways to Reuse Everyday Items.* Minneapolis: Millbrook Press, 2009.

Sivertsen, Tosh, and Linda Sivertsen. *Generation Green: The Ultimate Teen Guide to Living an Eco-Friendly Life.* New York: Simon Pulse, 2008.

RECYCLE

Internet Sites

FactHound offers a safe, fun way to find Internet sites related to this book. All of the sites on FactHound have been researched by our staff.

Here's all you do:

Visit *www.facthound.com*

FactHound will fetch the best sites for you!

Index

About the Author

Carol Sirrine is a former elementary classroom, music, and art teacher. In 1988, she founded ArtStart, an organization that combines learning in the arts with environmental stewardship. ArtStart's ArtScraps, located in St. Paul, Minnesota, combines waste management with art making. In a unique partnership with businesses and manufacturers, ArtScraps collects scraps, overstock, factory rejects, and other items normally destined for the landfill. These products are made available to teachers, parents, artists, Scout leaders, and day-care providers.